Amazing Art! Lesson Plans for Grades 6-12

Written by:

Christina Berretta

Copyright © 2018 Christina Berretta

All rights reserved.

ISBN:1985874946
ISBN-13: 978-1985874947

*This book is dedicated to my dearest friend and mentor
Georgina Ennis*

Artist Statement

For the past 14 years, I have asked my students on the first day of school, "What word is hiding in heart?" "ART!" They respond. Yes, art comes from your heart. Another thing I say is, "There are no mistakes, so you don't be self-conscious." Art is your escape from this world and the outlet for your soul. Art is the vehicle to communicate with the world around you. "Draw every day! Draw from observation. Carry around your sketchbook and fill it with anything you find interesting. For example, sketches of people in central the park, collect ticket stubs, fabric swatches, nature, wrapping paper, ribbons, newspaper clippings, a picture from a magazine, etc… Draw something you've found."

What great joy I feel to share my love of art history & art making with my students. I show my students the work of the masters and demonstrate techniques. I allow students space to find their own voices. For me, art making is a life- long journey. Every part of my life I draw from. That makes great personal art. As the years pass, more knowledge is gained, experiences & memories fill my mind. Visiting museums, reading about artists, watching movies, eating food, talking with friends, and everyday life tasks add to my art making. The more I expose myself to art in all mediums, the better I understand it. I can never learn enough. If I knew it all, my art would be stagnant.

For me, Art a is free- form, an emotional, spontaneous experience. I have noticed that when I focus on drawing I limit myself. I tell my students to be open to all mediums and take risks. For me, the best art takes place when you're not thinking about every mark you are putting on the blank sheet of paper. For example, while I am silk-screening, I listen to music. I'm in the art zone! When I play the drums with my band, I'm creating music. It is a great feeling to create and share with the world around you.

I have written over 4,000 original lesson plans. I have published this book of my favorite ones to inspire other teachers.

Remember that teaching is a vocation. There will be great days, good days, bad days, horror shows, and days that words can't describe. I pray every day for my students and ask the Lord to guide me. Share your talents with your students and may God be with you on the road of teaching.

You can visit my website to view my personal artwork www.christinaberretta.com

- Christina

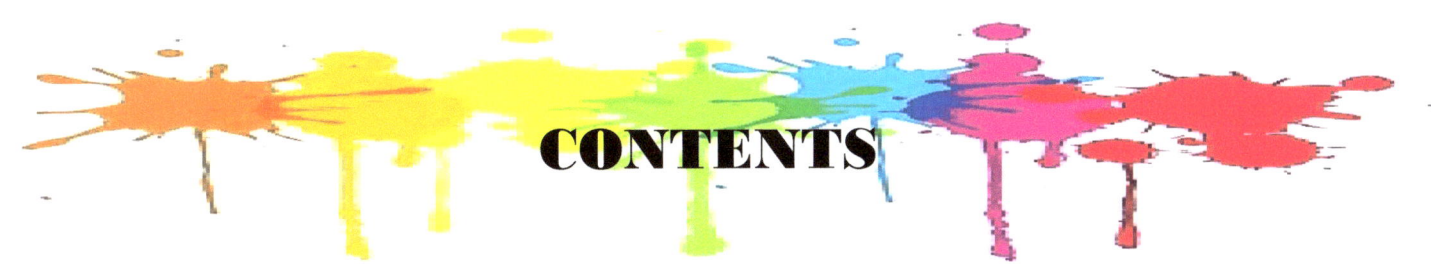

CONTENTS

What is Value?

Basic Drawing Unit

Shading Techniques Hatching, Cross-Hatching, & Stippling

Drawing 3D Forms: Cone, Cube, Cylinder, Sphere, Rectangle

Observational Drawing Shoes, Hats, & Still Life Objects

Alex Katz: Drawing & Painting Portraits

Figure Drawing 30 second exercises & long poses

Henri Matisse Still Life Collage

Color Theory

Perspective

Advanced Perspective: Figures in a Space

Landscapes

Drawing & Painting A Masterwork

Rubric & Student Self-Assessment Worksheets

Basic Drawing Unit

AIM: What is Value?

MATERIALS: pencils, paper, folders, # cards to assign seats & closet spaces, routines and expectations chart, rubrics, student contact sheet, value worksheets, crayons, chalk pastels, colored pencils, sample value scales, plastic wine glasses, lamp, sample glass arrangement, charts, and posters.

VOCABULARY:
Value – is the lightness or darkness of a color
Hue- color
Still life- non-living objects

MINI LESSON: Exploring Value
- Explain and demonstrate to the students that innumerous values live inside one pencil/crayon/chalk pastel/paint etc…
- Using only a pencil, create a value scale from light to dark
- Students work independently on the do now worksheet/sketchbook
- Check and monitor student progress

STUDENT WORKSHOP:
Day One and Day Two: Drawing from Observation
- Place a plastic wine glass on your desk/look at the still life arrangement in front of the room
- Observe how the light source shines onto the plastic glass (from the right, left, center, etc…)
- Notice the different number of values on the glass
- Draw the plastic glass from observation
- Using your pencil only, shade in all the lights and darks on the plastic glass
- Put your plastic glass (figure) in a space
- Draw the table the glass is sitting on
- Apply the values to the table and background

Day Three: Framing & Student Rubric & Reflection
- Trace and cut a construction paper frame
- Place and tape your artwork inside the frame
- Write your name on the back of your drawing and clean up
- Complete self-assessment reflection/rubric

SHARE:
- Students will present their work to the class
- Students will explain in their own words how to make a value scale & apply it to a figure

SELF ASSESSMENT REFLECTION/RUBRIC:
What is value? How did I as a student make a value scale?
StudentReflection:_____

Self-Assessment Score Scale	Craftsmanship	Effort	Thinking Skills

ART RUBRIC

Score	Craftsmanship & Creativity	Effort	Thinking Skills
A+ 97-100 A 93-96 A- 90-92	Very Unique Creative use of materials Creative Expression Extreme attention to details Mastery of value & art techniques taught Personal interpretation	Superior use of class time Treats materials with respect Works independently when necessary & collaborates with classmates	Exceptional problem solving skills Executes proposed ideas Superior comprehension of art history, art making & technical process
B+ 87-89 B 83-86 B- 80-82	Very good use of materials and attention to detail evidence of personal expression and interpretation	Focused on project Used class time well Worked independently when necessary & collaborates with classmates	Shows understanding of problem given Good comprehension of art history, art making & technical process
C+ 77-79 D 69-65	Completed the assignment Satisfactory attention to detail Some personal expression	Not on task all the time Rarely asked for help Rushed through assignment Didn't follow the directions given	Minimum amount of work in planning and executing Barely shows understanding of vocabulary, art skills and technical processes learned
F 64-55	Poor use of materials No personal expression Incomplete assignment Didn't use any art elements, principles of design, or techniques learned	Off task Breaking property Refuses help or guidance Does not ask questions or follow directions	Poor attention span during class discussion/mini lesson Doesn't plan/sketch ideas No understanding of methods, techniques or vocabulary

Basic Drawing Unit 1: Exploring Value

Vocabulary:

Value – is the lightness or darkness of a color

Hue – color

Do Now: Using only a pencil, create a value scale from light to dark.

Assignment:

- Place a plastic wine glass on your desk/look at the still life arrangement in front of the room
- Observe how the light source shines onto the plastic glass (from the right, left, center, etc...)
- Notice the different number of values on the glass
- Draw the plastic glass from observation
- Using your pencil only, shade in all the lights and darks on the plastic glass
- Put your plastic glass (figure) in a space
- Draw the table the glass is sitting on
- Apply the values to the table and background
- Trace and cut a construction paper frame
- Place and tape your artwork inside the frame
- Write your name on the back of your drawing
- Clean up

Shading Techniques Hatching, Cross-Hatching, & Stippling

AIM: What are the drawing techniques Hatching, Cross-Hatching, & Stippling?

MATERIALS: drawing paper, pencils, sample still life objects arrangement, pictures of still life objects, lamp, worksheets, ebony pencils, colored pencils, scissors, glue sticks, construction paper frames, and frame stencils.

VOCABULARY:
Hatching- a shading technique in which you make a series parallel strokes placed close together
Cross hatching- a shading technique in which you make a series of crisscrossed hatching strokes
Stippling - The act of stippling involves covering an area with dots. *The resulting image contains no lines.* It is a collection of dots, strategically placed to suggest forms, shapes, contrast and depth
Gradating- (from light to dark) apply heavy pressure on the side of your pencil and gradually lighten the pressure as you make your strokes.

MINI LESSON: How can I apply Hatching, Cross-Hatching, & Stippling to my drawing?
- Demonstrate Hatching, Cross-Hatching, & Stippling shading techniques
- When you see a very dark area, apply heavy pressure to achieve dark hatch marks
- When you see a very light area, apply little pressure to achieve light hatch marks
- Stippling marks are tightly packed together and vary in pressure and value
- Try the three types of shading techniques on your worksheet

STUDENT WORKSHOP: Drawing a still composition using shading techniques
- Choose 3 to 5 objects from the still life arrangement to sketch
- Draw what you see /observe all the contours
- Notice all the light and dark areas on each of the objects
- Choose one of the three styles of shading to apply to the still life arrangement
- Note: If you choose Stippling, begin your drawing with dots only (no lines)
- Use a pencil to make all the values
- Create a space for the objects (table, floor, shelf, etc…) to live in
- Trace and cut a paper frame
- Place and tape your work inside the frame
- Write your name
- Clean up

SHARE:
- Students will present their work to the class
- Students will explain in their own words the drawing techniques Hatching, Cross-Hatching, & Stippling

SELF ASSESSMENT REFLECTION/RUBRIC:
Which of the following drawing techniques (Hatching, Cross-Hatching, or Stippling) did you find the most difficult and why?
StudentReflection:_____
_____
_____

Self-Assessment Score	Craftsmanship	Effort	Thinking Skills

Shading Techniques: Hatching, Cross-Hatching, & Stippling

VOCABULARY:
Hatching- a shading technique in which you make a series parallel strokes placed close together
Cross hatching- a shading technique in which you make a series of crisscrossed hatching strokes
Stippling - The act of stippling involves covering an area with dots. *The resulting image contains no lines.* It is a collection of dots, strategically placed to suggest forms, shapes, contrast and depth
Gradating- (from light to dark) apply heavy pressure on the side of your pencil and gradually lighten the pressure as you make your strokes.

Do Now: Try the three types of shading techniques on your worksheet

Hatching	**Cross hatching**	**Stippling**

Assignment:
Drawing a Still Life Composition Using Shading Techniques

- Choose 3 to 5 objects from the still life arrangement to sketch
- Draw what you see /observe all the contours
- Notice all the light and dark areas on each of the objects
- Choose one of the three styles of shading to apply to the still life arrangement
- Note: If you choose Stippling, begin your drawing with dots only (no lines)
- Use a pencil to make all the values
- Create a space for the objects (table, floor, shelf, etc…) to live in
- Trace and cut a paper frame
- Place and tape your work inside the frame

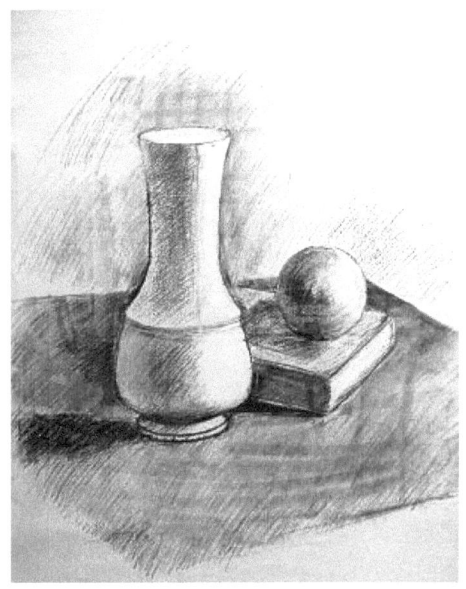

Drawing 3D Forms: Cone, Cube, Cylinder, Sphere, Rectangle

AIM: What is light intensity?

MATERIALS: pencils, paper, charcoal, chalk-pastels, crayons, colored pencils, lamp, 3D shape still life arrangement, 3D forms worksheet, value worksheet, viewfinders, glue sticks, scissors, and viewfinders.

MINI LESSON: Review What is value? / Making a value scale
- Value is the lightness or darkness of a color
- There are innumerous values inside one pencil, crayon, pastel, etc...
- Vary the pressure of your crayon, pencil, etc... to create a value scale 1-5
- 1 is the brightest and 5 is the darkest
- Fill in value scale worksheet with chalk pastels or crayons

STUDENT WORKSHOP: Drawing 3D forms
- Close the lights and turn on lamp to observe how the light falls on each 3D form
- Draw and Demonstrate to the class each shape separately
- Show how each value is applied to the forms
- Students practice drawing forms and values on worksheet
- Choose one crayon, pencil, or pastel to illustrate a composition of 5 forms or more on drawing paper
- Use only one value, one hue (color) (Example: many lights and darks of blue)
- Hold up your viewfinder to plan your composition
- Draw what you see (Look 90% at the objects and 10% at your paper)
- Create a background/environment for your 3D forms
- Cut out a frame for your artwork and glue it in place
- Write your name on the back and clean up

SHARE:
- Students will present their work to the class

- Students will explain in their own words how to make a value scale and apply it to 3D forms

SELF ASSESSMENT REFLECTION/RUBRIC:

StudentReflection:_____

Self-Assessment Score Scale	Craftsmanship	Effort	Thinking Skills

ART RUBRIC

Score	Craftsmanship & Creativity	Effort	Thinking Skills
A+ 97-100 A 93-96 A- 90-92	Very Unique Creative use of materials Creative Expression Extreme attention to details Mastery of value & art techniques taught Personal interpretation	Superior use of class time Treats materials with respect Works independently when necessary & collaborates with classmates	Exceptional problem solving skills Executes proposed ideas Superior comprehension of art history, art making & technical process
B+ 87-89 B 83-86 B- 80-82	Very good use of materials and attention to detail evidence of personal expression and interpretation	Focused on project Used class time well Worked independently when necessary & collaborates with classmates	Shows understanding of problem given Good comprehension of art history, art making & technical process
C+ 77-79 D 69-65	Completed the assignment Satisfactory attention to detail Some personal expression	Not on task all the time Rarely asked for help Rushed through assignment Didn't follow the directions given	Minimum amount of work in planning and executing Barely shows understanding of vocabulary, art skills and technical processes learned
F 64-55	Poor use of materials No personal expression Incomplete assignment Didn't use any art elements, principles of design, or techniques learned	Off task Breaking property Refuses help or guidance Does not ask questions or follow directions	Poor attention span during class discussion/mini lesson Doesn't plan/sketch ideas No understanding of methods, techniques or vocabulary

Value

Value – is the lightness or darkness of a color.

Pencil only

Red crayon or chalk pastel

Blue crayon or chalk pastel

Yellow crayon or chalk pastel

Light Intensity

3D Form	Right	Left	Center
Cone		↙ ↘	↓
Cube		↙ ↘	↓
Sphere		↙ ↘	↓
Cylinder		↙ ↘	↓
Rectangle		↙ ↘	↓

Observational Drawing Shoes

AIM: What is observational drawing?

MATERIALS: pencils, erasers, 9 x 12 newsprint paper, shoe still life arrangement, lamp, construction paper mats, frame stencils, scissors, glue, and shoe reference images.

MINI LESSON: What is a contour?
- the outline, the skeleton, the outer shell, the basic shape of your drawing
- It helps you frame out and plan the object/figure you are sketching

STUDENT WORKSHOP: Drawing shoes from observation
- Look at one of the shoe reference images or the shoes in the still life arrangement
- Notice and observe the line quality, details, logos, etc… on the shoe
- Sketch out the contour of the shoe
- Let the shoe take up the whole page (draw it as large as you can)
- Draw in all the details (stitching on the sneaker, logo, folds, creases, hanging shoelaces, etc…)
- Using a pencil, make a value scale from light to dark (1 to 5 values)
- Apply those values to the shoe you are sketching
- Put your shoe in a space (in the grass, gym floor, sidewalk, under the bed, etc…)
- Trace the fame stencil onto your construction paper
- Cut out the middle square only
- Drop the glue along the edge of your frame and place your drawing face down
- Write your name on the back and clean up

SHARE:
- Students will present their work to the class
- Students will explain in their own words what is observational drawing

DIFFERENTIATION:
- Students can design a sneaker from their imagination
- They can create their own logo and pose their shoe/shoes in an interesting composition.
- Students can take their own personal shoe off their foot and use that shoe to draw from

SELF ASSESSMENT REFLECTION/RUBRIC:
What is observational drawing? How did I as a student create a value scale, contours, and strengthen my observational drawing skills?
StudentReflection_____
_____

Self-Assessment Score Scale	Craftsmanship	Effort	Thinking Skills

ART RUBRIC

Score	Craftsmanship & Creativity	Effort	Thinking Skills
A+ 97-100 A 93-96 A- 90-92	Very Unique Creative use of materials Creative Expression Extreme attention to details Mastery of value & art techniques taught Personal interpretation	Superior use of class time Treats materials with respect Works independently when necessary & collaborates with classmates	Exceptional problem solving skills Executes proposed ideas Superior comprehension of art history, art making & technical process
B+ 87-89 B 83-86 B- 80-82	Very good use of materials and attention to detail evidence of personal expression and interpretation	Focused on project Used class time well Worked independently when necessary & collaborates with classmates	Shows understanding of problem given Good comprehension of art history, art making & technical process
C+ 77-79 D 69-65	Completed the assignment Satisfactory attention to detail Some personal expression	Not on task all the time Rarely asked for help Rushed through assignment Didn't follow the directions given	Minimum amount of work in planning and executing Barely shows understanding of vocabulary, art skills and technical processes learned
F 64-55	Poor use of materials No personal expression Incomplete assignment Didn't use any art elements, principles of design, or techniques learned	Off task Breaking property Refuses help or guidance Does not ask questions or follow directions	Poor attention span during class discussion/mini lesson Doesn't plan/sketch ideas No understanding of methods, techniques or vocabulary

Observational Drawing: Shoe Studies

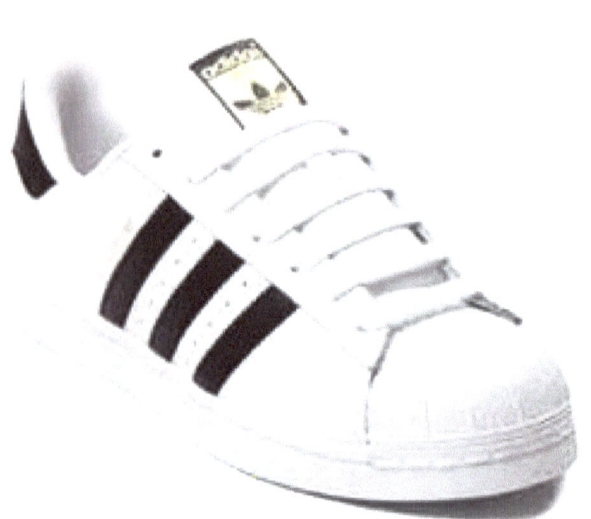 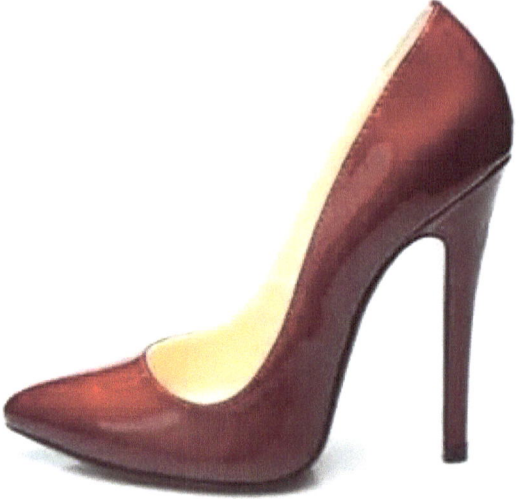

Vocabulary:

Contour - the outline, the skeleton, the outer shell, the basic shape of your drawing. It helps you frame out and plan the object/figure you are sketching.

Observational Drawing – drawing what you see/observe from life.

Value – is the lightness or darkness of a color

Do Now: Using only a pencil, create a value scale from light to dark.

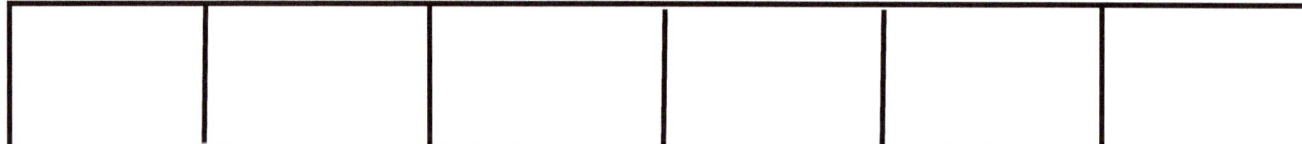

Assignment:

- Notice and observe the line quality, details, logos, etc… on the shoe
- Sketch out the contour of the shoe
- Let the shoe take up the whole page (draw it as large as you can)
- Draw in all the details (stitching on the sneaker, logo, folds, creases, hanging shoelaces, etc…)
- Using a piece of charcoal, make a value scale from light to dark (1 to 5 values)
- Apply those values to the shoe you are sketching
- Put your shoe in a space (in the grass, gym floor, sidewalk, under the bed, etc…)

Observational Drawing Hats

AIM: What is observational Drawing?

MATERIALS: pencils, erasers, 12 x 18 newsprint paper, Hat still life arrangement, lamp, foam mannequins, construction paper mats, frame stencils, scissors, glue, and hat reference images.

VOCABULARY: value, contour, observational drawing, still life, composition, hue, medium

MINI LESSON: What is value?

- Value – is the lightness or darkness of a color
- Using only a pencil, practice making a value scale on your do now worksheet/sketchbook

STUDENT WORKSHOP:

- Look at one of the hat reference images or the hats on display in the still life arrangement
- Notice and observe the line quality, details, ribbon, bow, lace, logos, etc… on the hat
- Sketch out the contours of the hat
- Let the hat take up the whole page (draw it as large as you can)
- Draw in all the details (stitching on the lid, logo, folds, creases, etc…)
- Using a pencil, make a value scale from light to dark (1 to 5 values)
- Apply those values to the hat you are sketching
- Put your hat in a space (on a mannequin, in the grass, gym floor, under the bed, etc…)
- Trace the fame stencil onto your construction paper
- Cut out the middle square only
- Drop the glue along the edge of your frame and place your drawing face down
- Smooth it out and clean off any glue drips
- Write your name on the back and clean up

DIFFERENTATION:

- Students can design a hat from their imagination
- They can create their own logo and pose their hat in an interesting composition
- Students can take their own personal hat and use that hat to draw from

SHARE:
- Students will present their work to the class
- Students will explain in their own words what is observational drawing

SELF ASSESSMENT REFLECTION/RUBRIC:

StudentReflection:_____

Self-Assessment Score	Craftsmanship	Effort	Thinking Skills

ART RUBRIC

Score	Craftsmanship & Creativity	Effort	Thinking Skills
A+ 97-100 A 93-96 A- 90-92	Very Unique Creative use of materials Creative Expression Extreme attention to details Mastery of value & art techniques taught Personal interpretation	Superior use of class time Treats materials with respect Works independently when necessary & collaborates with classmates	Exceptional problem solving skills Executes proposed ideas Superior comprehension of art history, art making & technical process
B+ 87-89 B 83-86 B- 80-82	Very good use of materials and attention to detail evidence of personal expression and interpretation	Focused on project Used class time well Worked independently when necessary & collaborates with classmates	Shows understanding of problem given Good comprehension of art history, art making & technical process
C+ 77-79 D 69-65	Completed the assignment Satisfactory attention to detail Some personal expression	Not on task all the time Rarely asked for help Rushed through assignment Didn't follow the directions given	Minimum amount of work in planning and executing Barely shows understanding of vocabulary, art skills and technical processes learned
F 64-55	Poor use of materials No personal expression Incomplete assignment Didn't use any art elements, principles of design, or techniques learned	Off task Breaking property Refuses help or guidance Does not ask questions or follow directions	Poor attention span during class discussion/mini lesson Doesn't plan/sketch ideas No understanding of methods, techniques or vocabulary

Observational Drawing: Hat Studies

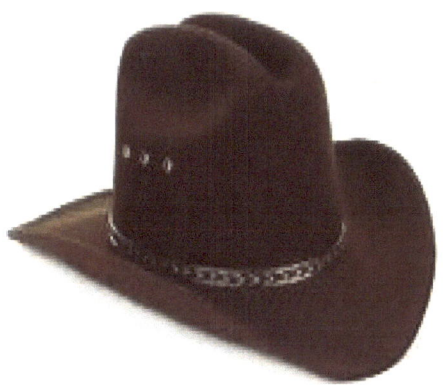

Vocabulary:

Contour - the outline, the skeleton, the outer shell, the basic shape of your drawing. It helps you frame out and plan the object/figure you are sketching.

Observational Drawing – drawing what you see/observe from life.

Value – is the lightness or darkness of a color

Do Now: Using only a pencil, create a value scale from light to dark.

Assignment:

- Notice and observe the line quality, details, logos, etc… on the hat/display of hats
- Sketch out the contour of the hat
- Let the hat take up the whole page (draw it as large as you can)
- Draw in all the details (stitching on the sneaker, logo, folds, creases, hanging shoelaces, etc…)
- Using a piece of charcoal, make a value scale from light to dark (1 to 5 values)
- Apply those values to the hat you are sketching
- Place your hat in a space (on the mannequin, in the grass, gym floor, sidewalk, under the bed, etc…)

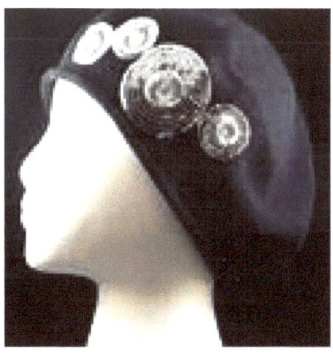

Observational Drawing Still Life

AIM: What is still life?

VOCABULARY:
Value – the lightness or darkness of a color
Still life – an arrangement of non-living objects
Positive space – the shape or figure in a design
Negative space – the empty space (white space)

MATERIALS: still life objects, desk lamp, colored pencils, crayons, chalk pastels, watercolor paints, brushes, towels, water jars, water, newsprint paper, construction paper frames, scissors, tape, glue, frame stencils, viewfinders, still life photos from picture collection, Janet Fish worksheets, Janet Fish posters, and pencils.

MINI LESSON: Who is Janet Fish?
- Janet Fish is an American contemporary artist.
- She makes all of her objects appear transparent and 3D by using different color values

STUDENT WORKSHOP: Creating a still life composition
- Read the worksheet about Janet Fish
- Look how she uses color values to create realistic still life objects in a space
- Choose 5 to 7 objects from the still life display to sketch or use still life photos from the picture collection
- Choose one crayon/colored pencil/chalk pastel/watercolor paints for your value scale
- Create a value scale from one the lightest to five the darkest
- Look and observe how the light from the lamp creates highlights and shadows on each of the objects
- (optional) Use your viewfinder to help you draw the objects from different views
- Apply the values from your scale to the still life objects based on your observations
- Trace and cut a frame
- Place and glue or tape or image in place
- Write your name on the back and clean up

SHARE:
- Students will present their work to the class
- Students will explain in their own words what is a still life and how to create many values using only one pencil/crayon/pastel/watercolor

SELF ASSESSMENT REFLECTION/RUBRIC:
StudentReflection:_____

Self-Assessment Score	Craftsmanship	Effort	Thinking Skills

Janet Fish

Janet Fish was born in 1939. She is an American contemporary artist. Look at her paintings below. She makes all of her objects appear transparent and three dimensional by using different color values. Janet Fish thinks of herself as a "painterly realist," primarily interested in light, atmosphere, motion and color. It is truly amazing. Here is a picture of Janet working in her New York City studio. She also has another studio in Middletown Springs, Vermont.

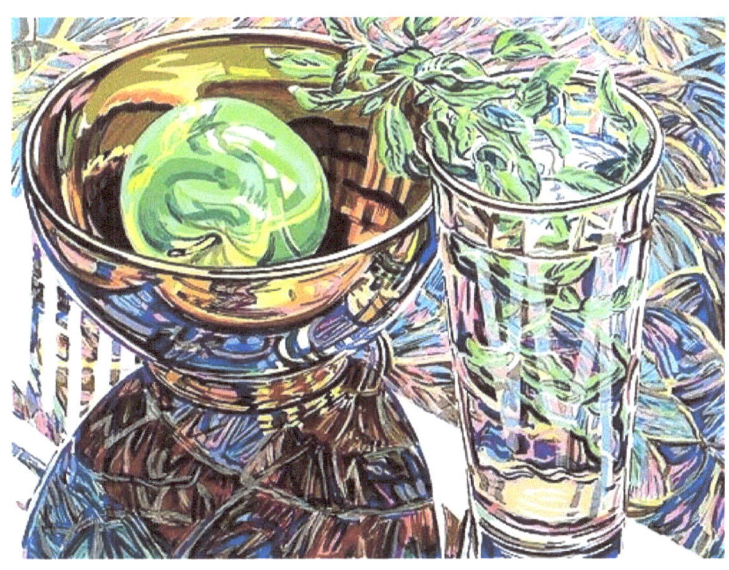

Assignment

Choose 5 to 7 objects from the still life display to sketch or use still life photos from the picture collection. Choose one crayon/colored pencil/chalk pastel to create a value scale. Look and observe how the light from the lamp creates highlights and shadows on each of the objects. Apply the values from your value scale to the still life objects based on your observations. Frame your work.

Vocabulary

Hue- color

Still life – an arrangement of non-living objects

Value- is the light ness or darkness of a color

Alex Katz: Drawing & Painting Portraits

AIM: Who is Alex Katz?

MATERIALS: Alex Katz reference color prints & books, watercolor paints, brushes, water cups, sketchbooks, paper towels, watercolor paper, frames, tape, and pencils

VOCABULARY: Crop, Magnify, Bleed, Overlap, Contrast, Balance

MINI LESSON: The Life & Work of Alex Katz
- **Alex Katz** born July 24, 1927, Sheepshead Bay, Brooklyn, New York,
- American figurative painter known for his large-scale simplified images of family and friends.
- Katz created iconic paintings documenting the American scene and later the American landscape through understated but monumental glimpses of the vernacular world.
- Katz's portraits create a tension between specific and abstract, intimate and remote, near and far.
- This tension animates Katz's depiction of both people and space.
- Katz's artistic style is a combination of movies, photography, and advertising.
- He dramatically crops and magnifies his portraits.

STUDENT WORKSHOP: Creating your own Alex Katz Art Piece
- Look at the work of Alex Katz.
- Notice the dramatic facial expressions and use of color.
- Choose one of his colored prints to draw and paint.
- (Optional) Create a Dramatic portrait of yourself using three descriptive words.
- For example: Serious, Funny, and Fashionable.
- What would your portrait look like?
- Draw from observation using one of the photo references
- (Optional) Draw from your imagination
- Adorn your art piece with watercolors
- Frame your work
- Clean up

DIFFERENTATION: Students having difficulty drawing the Alex Katz portraits from observation/imagination can create their own abstraction.

SHARE:
- Students will present their work to the class
- Students will explain in their own words who was Alex Katz

SELF ASSESSMENT REFLECTION/RUBRIC:

StudentReflection:_____

Self-Assessment Score	Craftsmanship	Effort	Thinking Skills

ART RUBRIC

Score	Craftsmanship & Creativity	Effort	Thinking Skills
A+ 97-100 A 93-96 A- 90-92	Very Unique Creative use of materials Creative Expression Extreme attention to details Mastery of value & art techniques taught Personal interpretation	Superior use of class time Treats materials with respect Works independently when necessary & collaborates with classmates	Exceptional problem solving skills Executes proposed ideas Superior comprehension of art history, art making & technical process
B+ 87-89 B 83-86 B- 80-82	Very good use of materials and attention to detail evidence of personal expression and interpretation	Focused on project Used class time well Worked independently when necessary & collaborates with classmates	Shows understanding of problem given Good comprehension of art history, art making & technical process
C+ 77-79 D 69-65	Completed the assignment Satisfactory attention to detail Some personal expression	Not on task all the time Rarely asked for help Rushed through assignment Didn't follow the directions given	Minimum amount of work in planning and executing Barely shows understanding of vocabulary, art skills and technical processes learned
F 64-55	Poor use of materials No personal expression Incomplete assignment Didn't use any art elements, principles of design, or techniques learned	Off task Breaking property Refuses help or guidance Does not ask questions or follow directions	Poor attention span during class discussion/mini lesson Doesn't plan/sketch ideas No understanding of methods, techniques or vocabulary

Alex Katz

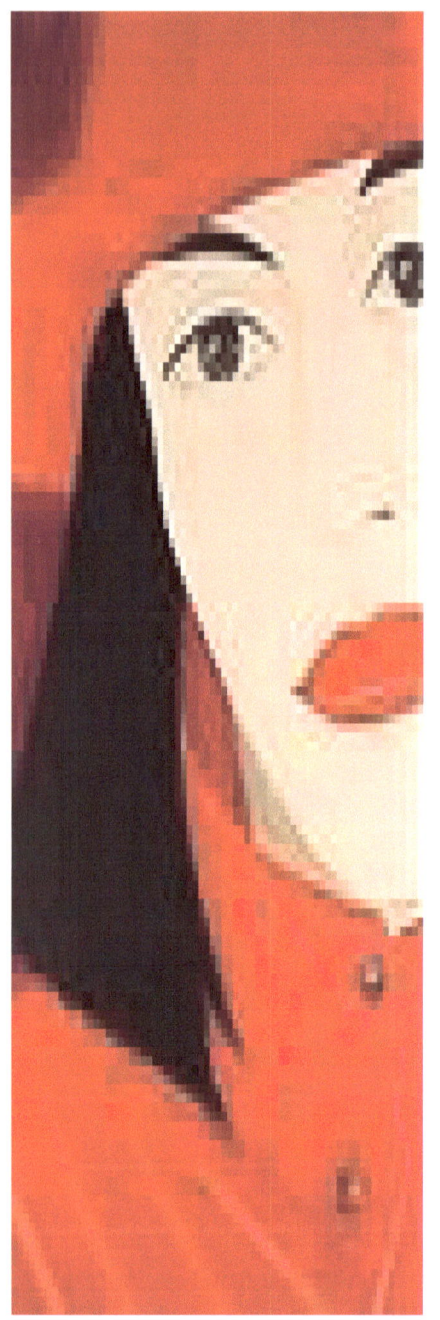

Alex Katz was American figurative painter known for his large-scale simplified images of family and friends. Katz created iconic paintings that were glimpses of the everyday world. Katz's portraits created contrast between specific and abstract, intimate and remote, near and far. "Red Coat", (on your left), is a portrait of his wife Ada. Katz's artistic style is a combination of movies, photography, and advertising. He dramatically crops and magnifies his portraits. The portrait below is called "Face of a Poet".

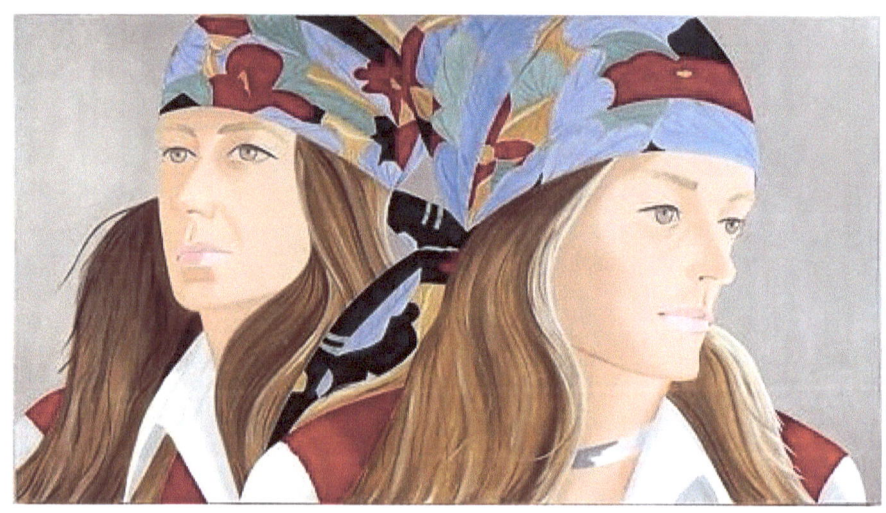

Assignment:

Look at the work of Alex Katz. Notice the dramatic facial expressions and use of color. Choose one of his colored prints to draw and paint. (Optional) Create a Dramatic portrait of yourself using three descriptive words. For example: Serious, Funny, and Fashionable. What would your portrait look like?

Figure Drawing 30 Second Exercises & Long Poses

AIM: What is Figure Drawing?

MATERIALS: wooden model, figure drawing worksheets, lamp, scrap paper, base, stumps, black cloth for backdrop, charcoal, pencils, white paper, viewfinders, scissors, tape, timer, glue, frame stencils, large construction paper.

MINI LESSON: Warm Up Exercise 30 second Gesture Sketches
- Pose the model
- Set the timer for 30 seconds
- Look only at the model and sketch in the whole body without details
- Look at the movement of the body and render it as best as you can
- This technique will help prepare you to sketch out figures/objects quickly and accurately
- Read and discuss the figure worksheet as a class

STUDENT WORKSHOP: Drawing the Wooden Model
- Look at the figure posed with the lamp light on and the shadows cast on the backdrop
- Use your viewfinder to create an interesting composition
- Sketch out what you see in pencil lightly
- With the charcoal, make many values of black
- Use the stump to blend the shaded areas of charcoal
- Trace and cut out a frame for your work
- Glue your work inside your frame
- Write your name on the back and clean up

SHARE:
- Students will present their work to the class
- Students will explain in their own words how to draw the wooden figure

SELF ASSESSMENT REFLECTION/RUBRIC:
StudentReflection:_____

Self-Assessment Score	Craftsmanship	Effort	Thinking Skills

Figure Drawing

30 Second Gesture Sketches

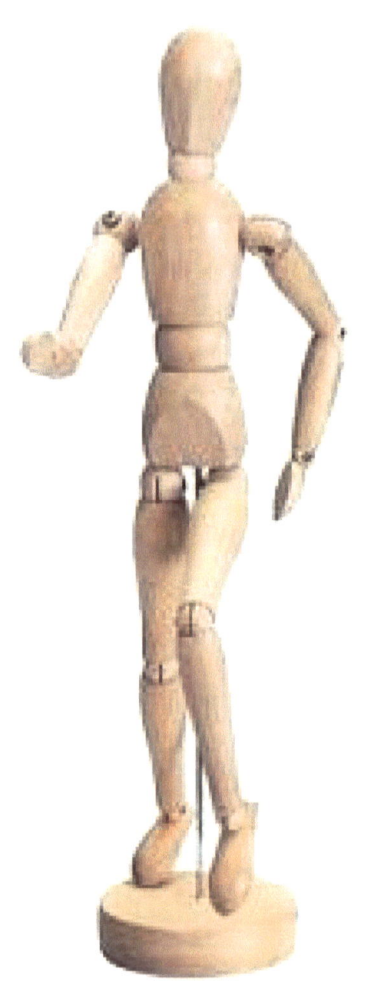

Pose the model

Set the timer for 30 seconds

Look only at the model and sketch in the whole body without details (hair, eyes, nose, mouth, etc...)

Look at the movement of the body and render it as best as you can

This technique will help prepare you to sketch out figures/objects quickly and accurately

Vocabulary Words:

Gesture Sketch – drawing the movement or position of a figure

Value – the lightness or darkness of a color

Henri Matisse Still Life Collage

AIM: What is a collage?

MATERIALS: 8 1/2 by 11 drawing paper, Posters & books of Henri Matisse, photo references, viewfinders, worksheets, creating a composition worksheets, frames, Manila paper, collage paper, scissors, glue, felt pieces, construction paper, glue, and pencils

VOCABULARY:
Collage - an artwork made up of bits & pieces of two-dimensional materials pasted to a surface.
Composition –describes the organization of (positive and negative) space in a picture.
Symmetrical – the same on both sides
Asymmetrical – different on both sides
Still Life – an arrangement of non-living objects

MINI LESSON: Who was Henri Matisse?
- 20th century French painter
- He became bedridden and needed a wheel chair to get around
- He devoted his time and energy to this new medium
- When he was 74, he created compositions from cut painted paper
- He enjoyed "drawing with his scissors"
- Notice how his designs are simple & mysterious

STUDENT WORKSHOP:
Day One to Day Three: Creating a Still life collage
- Pick 5 to 7 objects for your still life collage or create your own Matisse inspired collage
- Choose any fabric, collage paper, ribbon, etc… to create the figures in your composition
- Cut up pieces of construction paper to illustrate the objects
- use simple symmetry to create the objects
- Fold a paper in half and draw half of the object
- Cut on the line and open the paper up to reveal a symmetrical shape
- Place the objects in a space
- Create a colorful a background and glue your objects in place

Day Four: Framing & Self-Assessment Reflection Rubric
- Measure and cut out a frame
- Write your name on the back, & clean up

SHARE:
- Students will present their work to the class
- Students will explain in their own words what is a collage & who is Henri Matisse

SELF ASSESSMENT REFLECTION/RUBRIC:
What is a collage?
StudentReflection:_____
_____

Self-Assessment Score Scale	Craftsmanship	Effort	Thinking Skills

ART RUBRIC

Score	Craftsmanship & Creativity	Effort	Thinking Skills
A+ 97-100 A 93-96 A- 90-92	Very Unique Creative use of materials Creative Expression Extreme attention to details Mastery of value & art techniques taught Personal interpretation	Superior use of class time Treats materials with respect Works independently when necessary & collaborates with classmates	Exceptional problem solving skills Executes proposed ideas Superior comprehension of art history, art making & technical process
B+ 87-89 B 83-86 B- 80-82	Very good use of materials and attention to detail evidence of personal expression and interpretation	Focused on project Used class time well Worked independently when necessary & collaborates with classmates	Shows understanding of problem given Good comprehension of art history, art making & technical process
C+ 77-79 D 69-65	Completed the assignment Satisfactory attention to detail Some personal expression	Not on task all the time Rarely asked for help Rushed through assignment Didn't follow the directions given	Minimum amount of work in planning and executing Barely shows understanding of vocabulary, art skills and technical processes learned
F 64-55	Poor use of materials No personal expression Incomplete assignment Didn't use any art elements, principles of design, or techniques learned	Off task Breaking property Refuses help or guidance Does not ask questions or follow directions	Poor attention span during class discussion/mini lesson Doesn't plan/sketch ideas No understanding of methods, techniques or vocabulary

Working with Color & Composition
Henri Matisse

Henri Matisse was a 20th century French painter. He became bedridden and needed a wheel chair to get around. When he was 74, he created compositions from cut painted paper. He devoted his time and energy to this new medium. He enjoyed "drawing with his scissors"

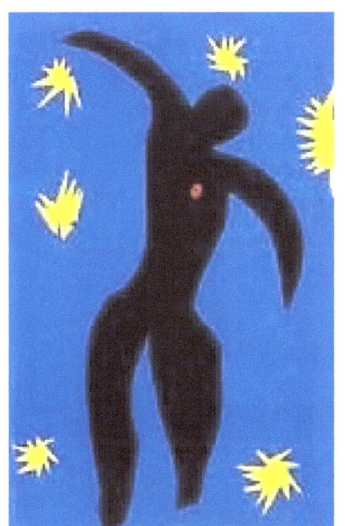 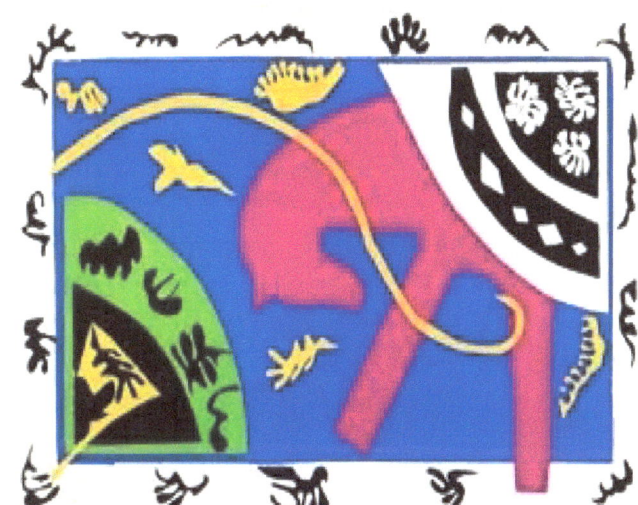 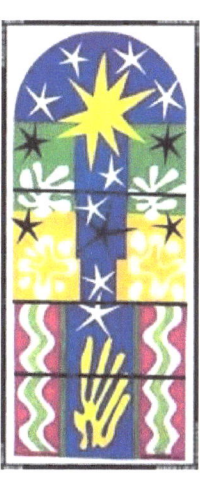

Assignment: Creating a Still Life collage

Pick 5 to 7 objects from the display for your still life collage or create your own Matisse inspired collage. Choose any fabric, collage paper, ribbon, etc… to create the figures in your composition. Cut up pieces of construction paper to illustrate the objects. Use symmetry to create the objects. Place the objects in a space. Create a colorful a background.

VOCABULARY:
Still Life – an arrangement of non-living objects
Collage - an artwork made up of bits & pieces of two-dimensional materials pasted to a surface.
Composition –describes the organization of (positive and negative) space in a picture.
Symmetrical – the same on both sides
Asymmetrical – different on both sides

Color Theory

AIM: What are the primary, secondary, and tertiary colors?

VOCABULARY:
Primary colors- red, yellow, & blue, cannot be made.
Secondary colors- green, violet (purple), orange are made by combining 2 primary colors
Tertiary colors- Red Violet, Blue Violet, Yellow Green, Blue Green, Yellow Orange, & Red Orange, are made using the secondary color combinations
Complementary Colors- are opposites on the color wheel Red & Green, Yellow & Purple, Blue & Orange. They fight for attention when standing next to one another.

MATERIALS: color wheel worksheet, color theory notes, posters of the color wheel, pre- bagged crayons/oil pastels of all colors needed for adorning the color wheel, & pencils

MINI LESSON: All Secondary & tertiary colors are made from the primary colors

- Red, Yellow, & Blue are the primary colors
- The primary colors live in the center nucleus of the color wheel
- You can make the entire color wheel using only these 3 colors
- Review Color theory worksheet as a class
- Mix the secondary colors on your worksheet using only the primary colors

STUDENT WORKSHOP: The Color Wheel

- Look at the reference posters of the color wheel and worksheets to help you understand color theory
- The top of the triangle is colored red
- The two bottom parts of the triangle are blue and yellow
- Next, you will branch out your secondary colors
- Red + yellow = orange
- Blue + yellow = green
- Blue + red = violet (purple)
- Then you will combine the neighboring secondary colors to create the tertiary colors
- Red + Orange = red orange, Red + Violet = red violet, Blue + Violet = blue violet, Blue + Green =blue green, Yellow + Green = yellow green, Yellow + Orange =yellow orange
- Now, look at your finished color wheel
- Notice that the Complementary Colors are opposites on the color wheel Red & Green, Yellow & Purple, Blue & Orange.
- They fight for attention when standing next to one another.
- Label all colors on the wheel using a pen or pencil
- Save all your Color theory worksheets in your portfolio for the Art exam

SHARE:
- Students will present their work to the class
- Students will explain in their own words how to mix colors

SELF ASSESSMENT REFLECTION/RUBRIC: List all the primary, secondary, and tertiary colors. List all the complementary colors (opposites on the color wheel)

StudentReflection_____

Self-Assessment Score	Craftsmanship	Effort	Thinking Skills

Score	Craftsmanship & Creativity	Effort	Thinking Skills
A+ 97-100 A 93-96 A- 90-92	Very Unique Creative use of materials Creative Expression Extreme attention to details Mastery of value & art techniques taught Personal interpretation	Superior use of class time Treats materials with respect Works independently when necessary & collaborates with classmates	Exceptional problem solving skills Executes proposed ideas Superior comprehension of art history, art making & technical process
B+ 87-89 B 83-86 B- 80-82	Very good use of materials and attention to detail evidence of personal expression and interpretation	Focused on project Used class time well Worked independently when necessary & collaborates with classmates	Shows understanding of problem given Good comprehension of art history, art making & technical process
C+ 77-79 D 69-65	Completed the assignment Satisfactory attention to detail Some personal expression	Not on task all the time Rarely asked for help Rushed through assignment Didn't follow the directions given	Minimum amount of work in planning and executing Barely shows understanding of vocabulary, art skills and technical processes learned
F 64-55	Poor use of materials No personal expression Incomplete assignment Didn't use any art elements, principles of design, or techniques learned	Off task Breaking property Refuses help or guidance Does not ask questions or follow directions	Poor attention span during class discussion/mini lesson Doesn't plan/sketch ideas No understanding of methods, techniques or vocabulary

Color Theory

Primary Colors – Red, Yellow, and Blue. They are pure colors from God's earth and cannot be mixed.

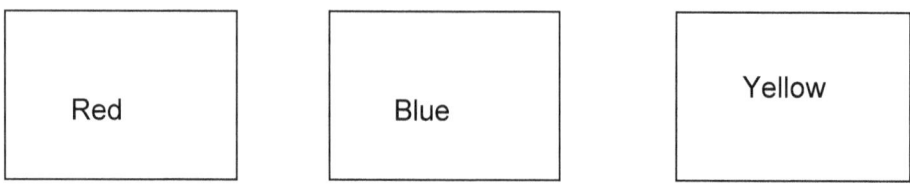

Secondary Colors – Green, Orange, and Purple (Violet). We mixed the primary colors to make the secondary colors.

Yellow + Blue = Green

Red + Yellow = Orange

Red + Blue = Purple (Violet)

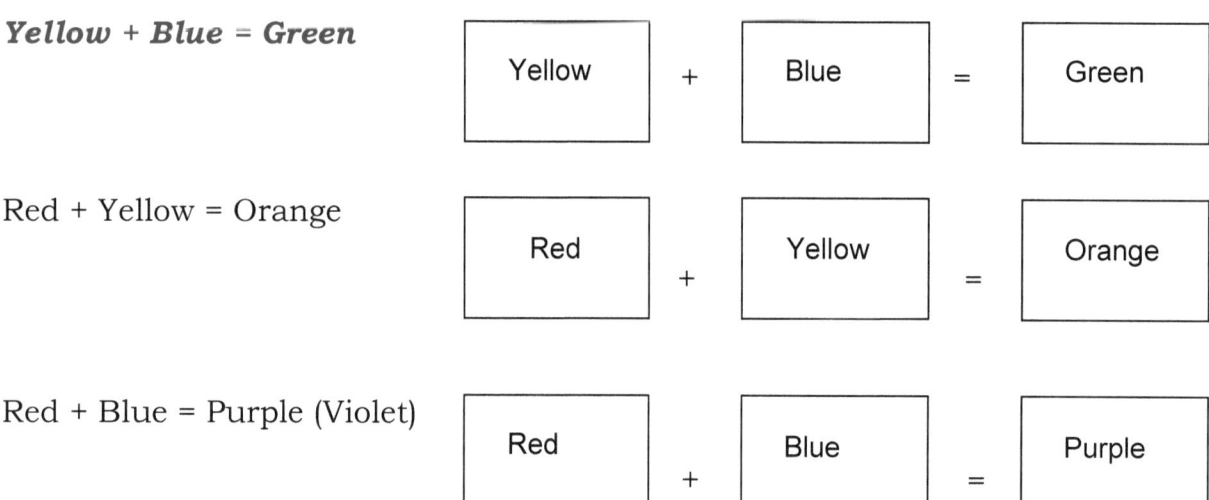

Complimentary Colors – Red & Green, Blue & Orange, Purple & Yellow

***They are opposites on the color wheel. When next to each other these vibrant colors fight for attention.

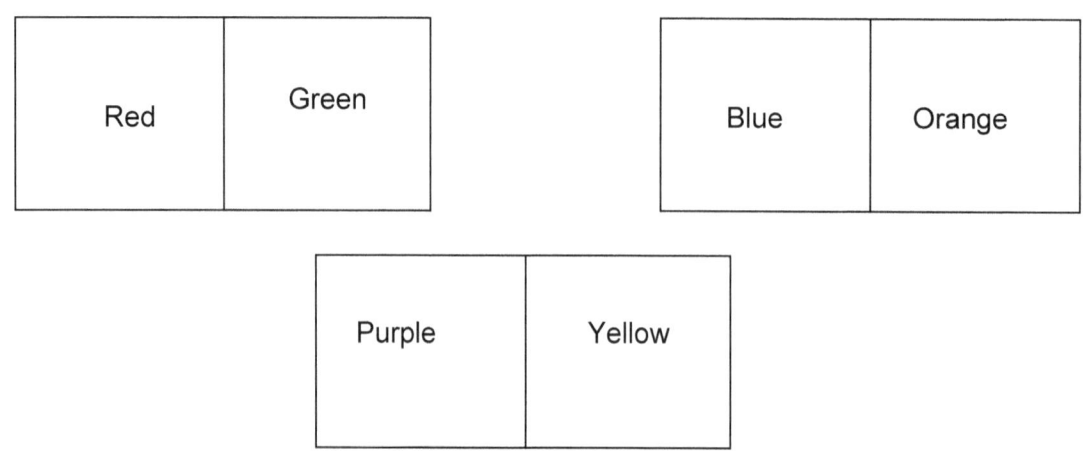

Tertiary Colors: We mixed the primary & secondary color pairs on the color wheel together to make the tertiary colors.

Red Orange   Red Violet   Yellow Orange   Yellow Green   Blue Green   Blue Violet

Part Two: Color Wheel

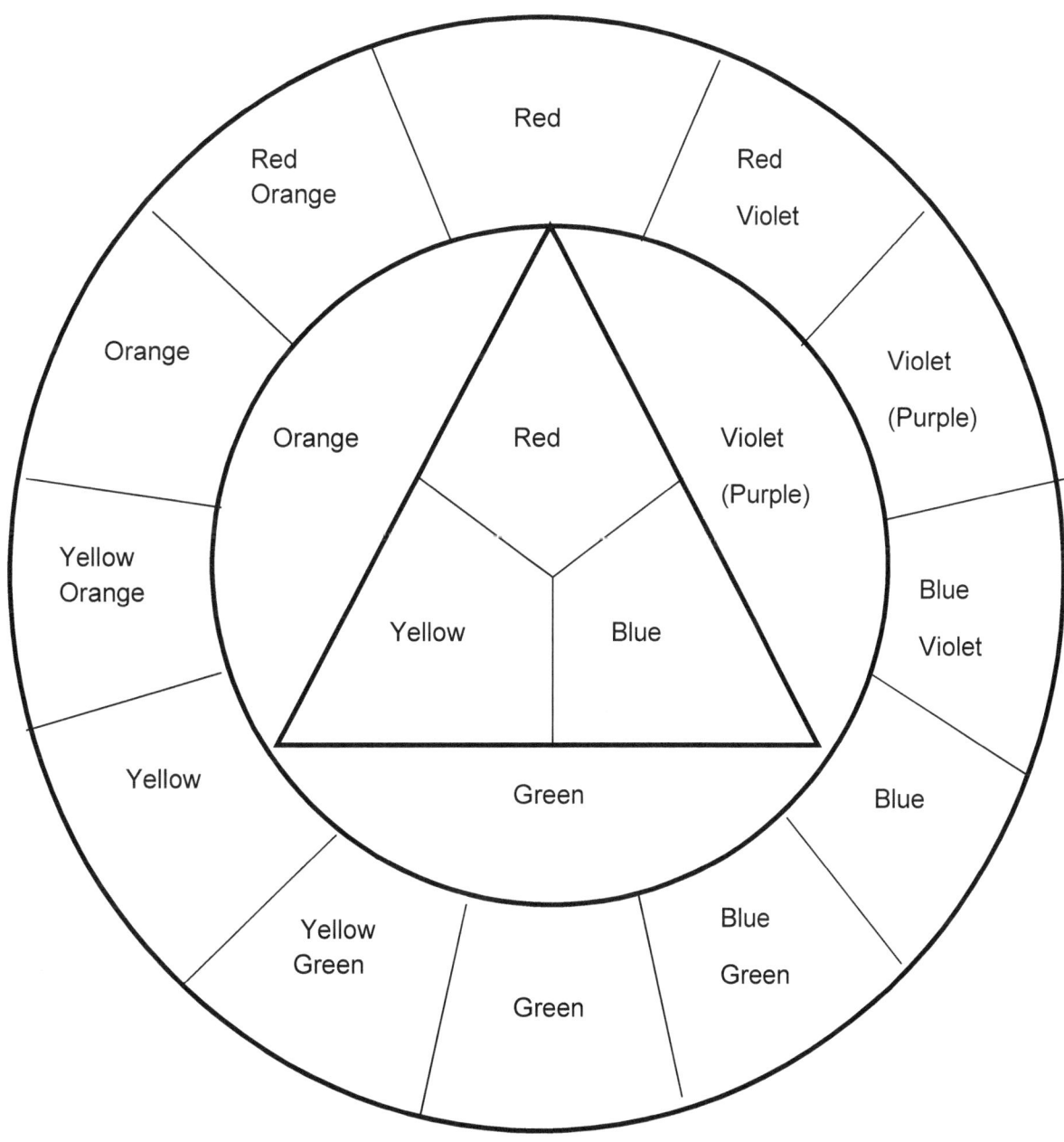

One Point Perspective

AIM: What is One Point Perspective?

VOCABULARY:
Diagonal Line - extending from one corner to the opposite corner
Vanishing point - is where parallel, straight, or angled lines meet on the horizon line.
Horizon Line – is a line marking the division of the earth and sky.
Vertical Line – a line rising straight up from a level surface
One Point Perspective – the means of arriving at a convincing two-dimensional drawing of the complex 3 dimensional world we perceive and inhabit.

MATERIALS: pencils, paper, rulers, colored pencils, markers, water color paints, paint brushes, watercolor paper, perspective worksheets, and oil pastels

MINI LESSON: Basic Rules of One Point Perspective
- Draw your vanishing point in the center of your page.
- Using your ruler, draw a horizontal line directly through the vanishing point.
- The vanishing point lives on the horizon line.
- Remember that all diagonal lines meet at the Vanishing Point.
- Keep in mind that the figures closest to the vanishing point are smaller and figures away from the vanishing point are larger.
- Master using and drawing diagonal lines on a 2 dimensional surface and you can create any 3 dimensional drawing!

STUDENT WORKSHOP: Drawing a city
- Draw a straight line across the page (horizon line)
- Put a big dot in the middle of the line (vanishing point)
- Demonstrate and explain one point perspective
- Read worksheet and use visual examples to set up proportions of objects in space
- Tilt your ruler 45 degrees and draw a slanted line (sidewalk)
- At the end of the slanted line draw a straight line (street)
- Add vertical lines to create tall buildings
- Draw a horizontal line to create train tracks above the buildings
- Draw in the windows, flower, gardens, buses, trains, etc…
- Color in your city with either paint or colored pencils
- Frame your work
- Write your name on the back

SHARE:
- Students will present their work to the class
- Students will explain in their own words what is one point perspective

SELF ASSESSMENT REFLECTION/RUBRIC:
What is One Point Perspective?
StudentReflection:_____

Self-Assessment Score	Craftsmanship	Effort	Thinking Skills

Art Rubric

Score	Craftsmanship & Creativity	Effort	Thinking Skills
A+ 97-100 A 93-96 A- 90-92	Very Unique Creative use of materials Creative Expression Extreme attention to details Mastery of value & art techniques taught Personal interpretation	Superior use of class time Treats materials with respect Works independently when necessary & collaborates with classmates	Exceptional problem solving skills Executes proposed ideas Superior comprehension of art history, art making & technical process
B+ 87-89 B 83-86 B- 80-82	Very good use of materials and attention to detail evidence of personal expression and interpretation	Focused on project Used class time well Worked independently when necessary & collaborates with classmates	Shows understanding of problem given Good comprehension of art history, art making & technical process
C+ 77-79 D 69-65	Completed the assignment Satisfactory attention to detail Some personal expression	Not on task all the time Rarely asked for help Rushed through assignment Didn't follow the directions given	Minimum amount of work in planning and executing Barely shows understanding of vocabulary, art skills and technical processes learned
F 64-55	Poor use of materials No personal expression Incomplete assignment Didn't use any art elements, principles of design, or techniques learned	Off task Breaking property Refuses help or guidance Does not ask questions or follow directions	Poor attention span during class discussion/mini lesson Doesn't plan/sketch ideas No understanding of methods, techniques or vocabulary

Vocabulary Words

Diagonal Line - extending from one corner to the opposite corner

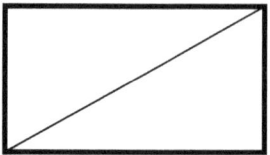

Vanishing point - the point in which all diagonal lines meet. The vanishing point lives on the horizon line

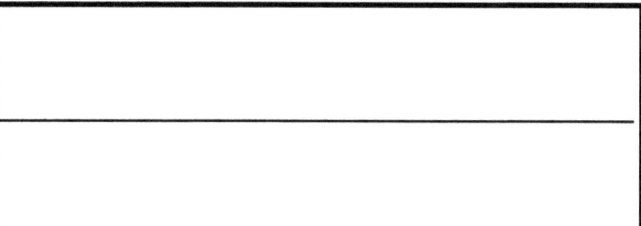

Horizon Line – is a line marking the division of the earth and sky.

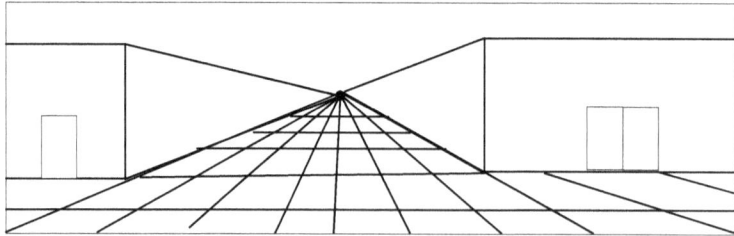

Vertical Line – a line rising straight up from a level surface

One Point Perspective – the means of arriving at a convincing two-dimensional drawing of the complex 3 dimensional world we perceive and inhabit.

Basic Rules of Perspective

- Draw your vanishing point in the center of your page.
- Using your ruler, draw a horizontal line directly through the vanishing point.
- The vanishing point lives on the horizon line.
- Remember that all diagonal lines meet at the Vanishing Point.
- Keep in mind that the figures closest to the vanishing point are smaller and figures away from the vanishing point are larger.
- Master using and drawing diagonal lines on a 2 dimensional surface and you can create any 3 dimensional drawing!

Drawing Your Own City Contest Rules

Must include a title and a theme. For example: "Candy Land" will have giant candies as buildings, chocolate rooftops, and licorice lakes, etc...

Must include people walking/running/exercising/playing/driving/eating/etc...

Must have details on signs, lamp posts, benches, brick walls, day/night skies, trees, flowers, billboards, bus stops, etc...

Must include at least one form of transportation. For example: helicopter, bus, train, bike, car, truck, RV, motorcycle, skateboard, boat, etc...

Use your imagination. Be creative and design your own restaurants/stores/etc...

Remember the rule: All lines go back to the vanishing point. Figures moving closest to the vanishing point are smaller. Figures moving away from the vanishing point are larger.

There will be only one set of 1st place, 2nd place, & 3rd place winners per grade level

Winners will be announced at the end of the class period and will claim their prize!

Good Luck to everyone!

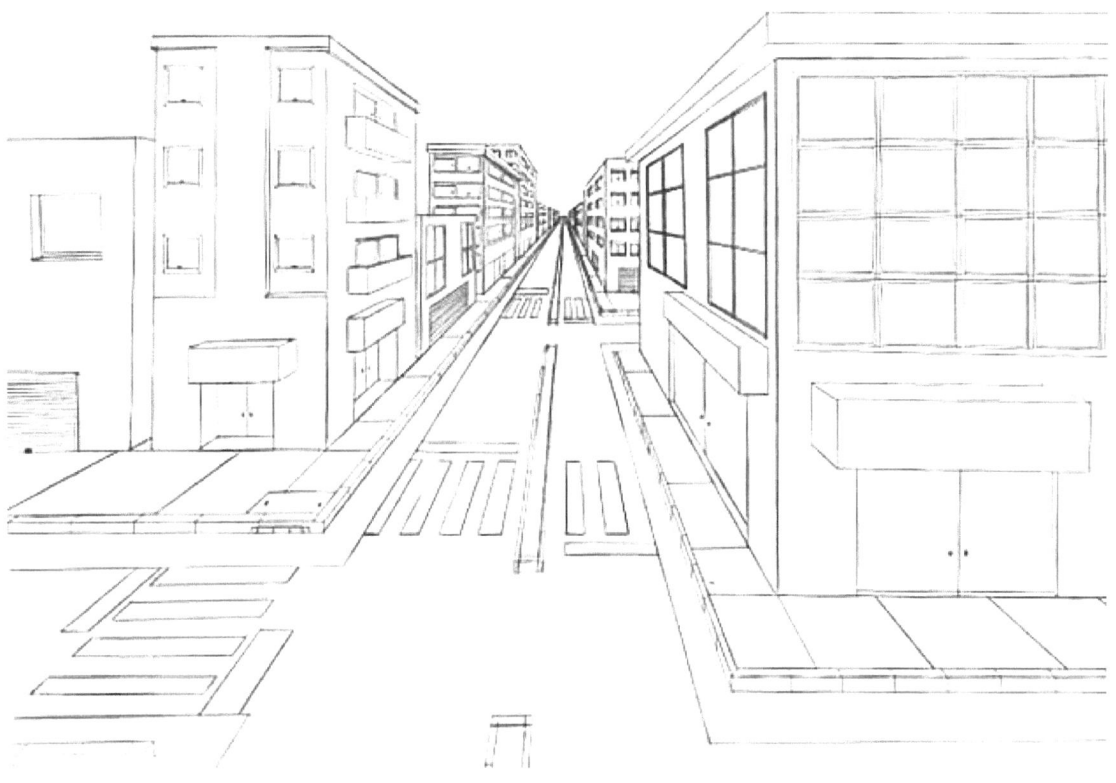

Try your best!

Advanced Perspective: Figures in a Space

AIM: How can I accurately draw a figure in a space?

VOCABULARY:
Trompe L´oeil (Tromp´- loy) - is a French term meaning "deception of the eye." It is a technique used so that a drawing/painting is photographically realistic. Master this technique and you may fool the viewer into thinking that the objects or scene represented are real rather than painted.

Linear Perspective is a mathematical system used to create an illusion of depth.

Vanishing Point - is where parallel, straight, or angled lines meet on the horizon line.

MATERIALS: drawing paper, pencils, construction paper frames, tape, glue, scissors, frame stencils, images of indoor and outdoor spaces, worksheets, Poster of Jos De Mey paintings, colored pencils, crayons, oil pastels, markers, and rulers.

MINI LESSON: The master of Deception: Jos De Mey
- Look at the work of Jos De Mey & read the worksheet
- Notice how he incorporated trompe l'oeil effects using highlight & shadow
- He made Paradoxical worlds (impossible worlds that are realistic and unrealistic)
- His early work was in furniture design & architecture
- In 1976, his works became more figurative and incorporated his figures into scenes
- He wanted to incorporate trompe l'oeil effects in his paintings.
- He was inspired by the work of M.C. Escher, Pieter Bruegel, and Rene Magritte

STUDENT WORKSHOP: Creating a figure in a space
- Read and Understand the concept of the trompe L`oeil technique
- Choose an image from the picture collection OR create your own figure in a space
- Sketch out the contours of all the figures
- Add in an additional human/animal figure to your scene example: cat on window sill, girl on couch, etc…
- Draw all the details of the couches, tables, windows, books, etc…
- Using a pencil, go back and add in the highlights and shadows as color shapes
- Color in your figures & objects with colored pencils, crayons, etc…
- Trace and Cut out a frame
- Glue or tape your drawing inside the frame
- Write your name on the back
- Clean up

SHARE:
- Students will present their work to the class
- Students will explain in their own words the drawing technique trompe l'oeil

SELF ASSESSMENT REFLECTION/RUBRIC:
How can I accurately draw a figure in a space?
StudentReflection:_____
_____

Self-Assessment Score	Craftsmanship	Effort	Thinking Skills

Score	Craftsmanship & Creativity	Effort	Thinking Skills
A+ 97-100 A 93-96 A- 90-92	Very Unique Creative use of materials Creative Expression Extreme attention to details Mastery of value & art techniques taught Personal interpretation	Superior use of class time Treats materials with respect Works independently when necessary & collaborates with classmates	Exceptional problem solving skills Executes proposed ideas Superior comprehension of art history, art making & technical process
B+ 87-89 B 83-86 B- 80-82	Very good use of materials and attention to detail evidence of personal expression and interpretation	Focused on project Used class time well Worked independently when necessary & collaborates with classmates	Shows understanding of problem given Good comprehension of art history, art making & technical process
C+ 77-79 D 69-65	Completed the assignment Satisfactory attention to detail Some personal expression	Not on task all the time Rarely asked for help Rushed through assignment Didn't follow the directions given	Minimum amount of work in planning and executing Barely shows understanding of vocabulary, art skills and technical processes learned
F 64-55	Poor use of materials No personal expression Incomplete assignment Didn't use any art elements, principles of design, or techniques learned	Off task Breaking property Refuses help or guidance Does not ask questions or follow directions	Poor attention span during class discussion/mini lesson Doesn't plan/sketch ideas No understanding of methods, techniques or vocabulary

Master of Deception: Jos De Mey

Jos De Mey painted paradoxical worlds onto his canvass. His paradoxical pictures of impossible worlds had realistic and unrealistic figures. However, Mey's earlier work was in furniture design & architecture. It wasn't until 1976, when his works became more figurative and incorporated his figures into scenes. He was inspired by the master works of M.C. Escher, Pieter Bruegel, and Rene Magritte. They too were masters of deception. How did they create these amazing paintings? They used Trompe l'oeil _(Tromp´- loy) It is a French term meaning "deception of the eye." It is a technique used so that a drawing/painting is photographically realistic. Master this technique and you may fool the viewer into thinking that the objects or scene represented are real rather than painted. Look at the work of Jos De Mey. Notice how he incorporated trompe l'oeil effects using highlight & shadow.

Assignment:

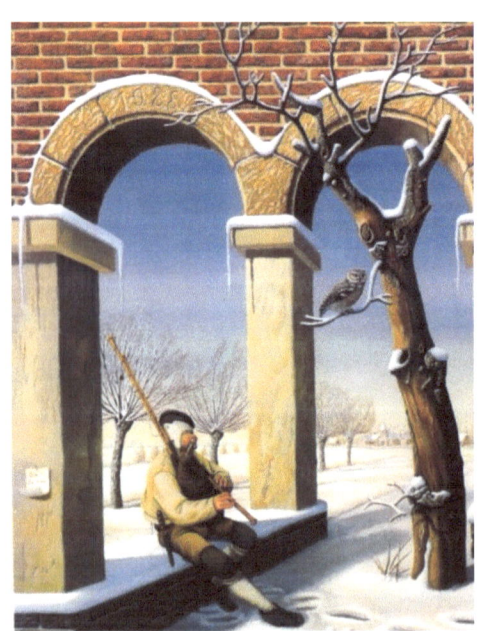

After reading and understanding the concept of the tromp l'oeil technique, choose an image from the picture collection to sketch. (Optional) You may create your own picture of a figure in a space. Sketch out all the contours of all the figures. Add an additional human/animal figure to your scene. For example, a cat is sleeping on the window sill, a girl sitting on the couch, etc... Draw all the details of the couches, windows, tables, books, etc... Go back and add in the highlights and shadows as color shapes.

Landscapes

AIM: What is a landscape?

MATERIALS: pencils, paper, frames, scissors, glue, tape, oil pastels, chalk pastels, colored pencils, and landscape reference pictures.

MINI LESSON: Review: Using the 7 elements of Design and One Point Perspective
- Line, shape, color, balance, scale, texture, pattern, & form.
- Vary the use of your lines, marks, brushstrokes, etc… to create variety
- One point perspective techniques (all lines meet at the vanishing point)
- Figures moving towards from the vanishing point are smaller
- Figures moving away from the vanishing point are larger

STUDENT WORKSHOP: Drawing a landscape from observation
- Choose an image from the picture collection
- Observe the distance between forms
- In pencil, sketch in the contours of all the plant life, water, hills, etc…
- Choose oil pastels, chalk, or colored pencils for your picture
- Make different types of strokes by rubbing gently
- Fill your whole page with bright colors
- Use different color values and outline some parts in black
- Cut out a construction paper frame
- Glue your picture inside the frame
- Write your name on the back and clean up

SHARE:
- Students will present their work to the class
- Students will explain in their own words why they chose to illustrate this landscape

SELF ASSESSMENT REFLECTION/RUBRIC:
StudentReflection:_____
_____
_____

Self-Assessment Score Scale	Craftsmanship	Effort	Thinking Skills

Assignment:
Drawing a landscape from observation

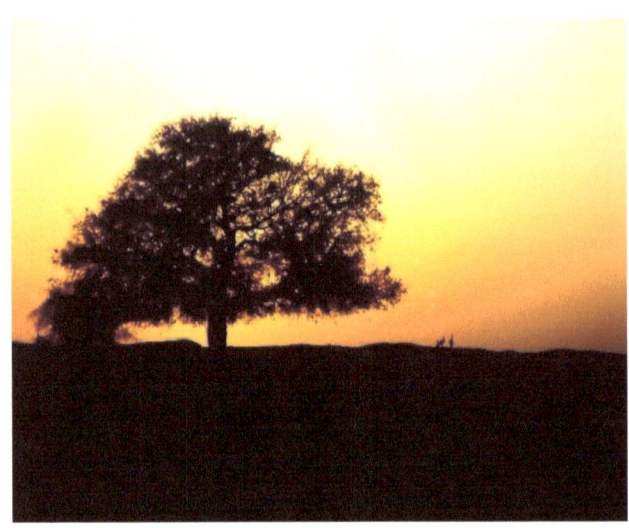 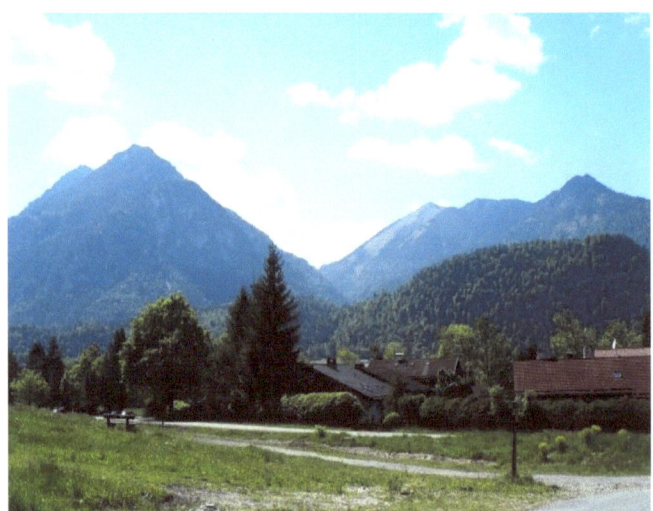

- Choose an image from the picture collection
- Observe the distance between forms
- In pencil, sketch in the contours of all the plant life, water, hills, etc...
- Choose oil pastels, chalk, or colored pencils for your picture
- Make different types of strokes by rubbing gently
- Fill your whole page with bright colors
- Use different color values and outline some parts in black
- Vary the use of your lines, marks, brushstrokes, etc... to create variety
- Remember to use One point perspective techniques (all lines meet at the vanishing point)
- Figures moving towards from the vanishing point are smaller
- Figures moving away from the vanishing point are larger
- Cut out a construction paper frame
- Glue your picture inside the frame
- Write your name on the back and clean up

Drawing & Painting A Masterwork

AIM: What is an art movement?

1st TVA A **trend within the Visual Arts** (a broad trend affecting the work of many artists)
2nd BCT A **broad cultural trend** (a term given to identify artwork and artists of that period)
3rd ADM **artist-defined movement** (artists that founded this type of art)
4th RAL **retrospectively applied label** (art historians who studied the art of that period and categorized it)

VOCABULARY: Impressionism, Modernism, Cubism, Futurism, Romanticism, Illusionism, Surrealism, Neo-Classicism, Realism, Abstract Expressionism

MATERIALS: pencils, crayons, oil pastels, watercolor paints, drawing paper, scissors, tape, frames, tracing paper, art timeline of movement/isms poster, guided response sample, worksheets, slide projector, slides, sketchbooks, art prints and posters.

MINI LESSON: Slideshow of Paintings: Understanding Movements and Isms
- Show the class a variety of paintings from the Renaissance to Post-Modernism (1300 A.D. to 2000 A.D.)
- Notice how art has developed and prospered over the years
- Choose a painting, print, sculpture, etc…from one of the movements/isms to illustrate & research

STUDENT WORKSHOP:
Day One: Slideshow of famous Artworks & Class Discussion
- Watch the slideshow of famous works of art we studied this year & other masterworks
- Show students art history cards, posters, and books about the artist's life & work they may use in their written report
- Choose one of the large prints from the picture collection
- Write the name of the painting and artist in your sketchbook
- Clip the painting of your choice to your Bristol board
- Write your name on your paint tray

Day Two to Day Three: Rendering a famous work of art
- Draw the painting as accurately as you can paying close attention the details
- Include all the lines, figures, background, etc…
- Remember to use all the techniques we learned and the elements of art
- Review color wheel and color theory when mixing acrylic paints

Day Four to Day Ten: Painting your Masterwork & Framing
- Adorn your picture with bright bold watercolors/acrylic paints
- Place your work face down inside the pre-cut frame and tape it in place
- Write your name on the back and clean up

Day Eleven and Day Twelve:
- Start your written portion of the end term project
- Copy the notes on the blackboard about all the art movements and vocabulary words in your sketchbook
- Use the plan sheet provided to help you write your paragraph
- Research the artist and painting you illustrated in class this month.
- Please define the art movement, state 3 facts about your artist, make 3 observations about the artist's painting, and explain why you chose this painting.
- This assignment should be one paragraph & completed on loose-leaf/inside your sketchbook

SHARE:
- Students will present their work to the class
- Students will explain why they chose this particular artist & painting

SELF ASSESSMENT REFLECTION/RUBRIC:
StudentReflection:_____
_____
_____

Self-Assessment Score	Craftsmanship	Effort	Thinking Skills

Rendering Famous Paintings, Prints, Sculptures, & Artifacts from the Renaissance to Post-Modernism (1300 A.D. to 2000 A.D.)

An **art movement** is...

1st TVA A **trend within the Visual Arts** (a broad trend affecting the work of many artists)
2nd BCT A **broad cultural trend** (a term given to identify artwork and artists of that period)
3rd ADM **artist-defined movement** (artists that founded this type of art)
4th RAL **retrospectively applied label** (art historians who studied the art of that period and categorized it)

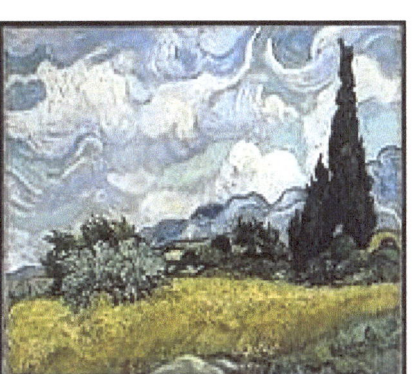 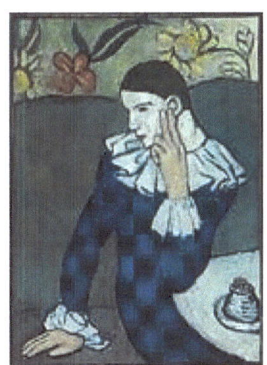 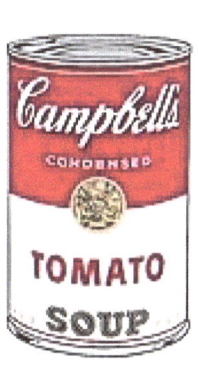 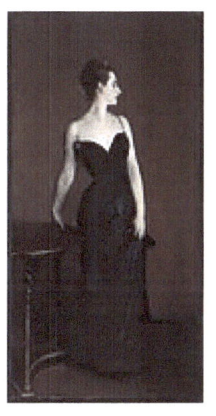 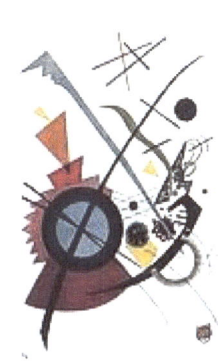

Assignment

As a class, watch the slideshow of famous paintings, prints, sculptures, & artifacts from around the world. Notice how the artwork has developed and prospered over the years. Choose a painting, print, sculpture, etc...from one of the movements/isms to illustrate & research. You will have one month to complete this end term project. First, you will sketch and paint a famous work of art. Then you will write a one page report about the artist.

SELF ASSESSMENT REFLECTION/RUBRIC:

Directions: State & answer the aim. What did you learn in this lesson/unit of study? Explain it in your own words. Use the rubric provided to evaluate your art project. Read the explanation of feedback for each individual column: craftsmanship and creativity, effort, and thinking skills

STUDENT REFLECTION:

_____

_____

_____

_____

Self-Assessment Score Scale	Craftsmanship & Creativity	Effort	Thinking Skills

ART RUBRIC

Score	Craftsmanship & Creativity	Effort	Thinking Skills
A+ 97-100 A 93-96 A- 90-92	Very Unique Creative use of materials Creative Expression Extreme attention to details Mastery of value & art techniques taught Personal interpretation	Superior use of class time Treats materials with respect Works independently when necessary & collaborates with classmates	Exceptional problem solving skills Executes proposed ideas Superior comprehension of art history, art making & technical process
B+ 87-89 B 83-86 B- 80-82	Very good use of materials and attention to detail evidence of personal expression and interpretation	Focused on project Used class time well Worked independently when necessary & collaborates with classmates	Shows understanding of problem given Good comprehension of art history, art making & technical process
C+ 77-79 D 69-65	Completed the assignment Satisfactory attention to detail Some personal expression	Not on task all the time Rarely asked for help Rushed through assignment Didn't follow the directions given	Minimum amount of work in planning and executing Barely shows understanding of vocabulary, art skills and technical processes learned
F 64-55	Poor use of materials No personal expression Incomplete assignment Didn't use any art elements, principles of design, or techniques learned	Off task Breaking property Refuses help or guidance Does not ask questions or follow directions	Poor attention span during class discussion/mini lesson Doesn't plan/sketch ideas No understanding of methods, techniques or vocabulary

Closing Statement

Thank you for purchasing my book. I included my original worksheets, general rubric, & self-assessment chart so you can make copies or feel free to create your own. As a teacher, you want to inspire the students to create art & share their talents with the community. Always be kind, clear, patient, and consistent. Start with what the students know and build on that. After that, encourage the students to leave their comfort zone and try new things.

Remember that a lesson plan is for the teacher! A lesson plan is an outline of your thoughts, materials, vocabulary, facts, etc… to teach your students the course material in a simple way. The material in the lesson plan is broken down so that the students can understand it, apply it, and own it. Don't let anyone undermine your teaching ability, tell you how to think, or insist that you need to fill out a nine page lesson plan.

Teaching is a vocation. It is a calling that God sent you to teach his children. Be patient with the students who break your crayons, waste your paint, try your patience, push your buttons, defy you, cause havoc, sit on your last nerve, and give your heartburn. The troubled students are the ones who need you the most! Pray for them every day and teach them kindness. By your good example, the students learn best. There will be awesome days, great days, good days, bad days, days that never end, and days that words can't describe the horror show you've endured. Hang in there.

The troubled students may not show it right now, but they care about what you think. Remember, they want positive recognition and rules. 10 years from now, you will run into a student who will to tell you….I miss your class….you made a difference in my life…

www.ingramcontent.com/pod-product-compliance
Lightning Source LLC
Chambersburg PA
CBHW051220220526
45473CB00003B/1105